Fresh Light

Poetry & Prose

"A fresh voice. Sharp, thoughtful, poignant, both tender and crisp."

Donna Minkowitz, author of "Donnaville", donnaminkowitz.com

"I sat down by a fireplace, a tall clock ticking nearby, and made my way into a terrific collection of poems, *Fresh Light*, by Jim Seegert. It was summer, so the fire wasn't lit, but Jim's words warmed my heart. His memories, in these poems, are precise retellings, and that makes for great art. He goes from Chinatown to Flagstaff, Arizona, in one beautiful fell swoop. His journey through fixing his kitchen becomes ours. We end up at the Seaport Museum and wave goodbye to him as he retires to the Hudson Valley, leaving behind all these fantastic constructs. This is an amazing book!"

Ron Kolm, contributing editor of Sensitive Skin. His books include A Change in the Weather, Welcome to the Barbecue and The Bookstore Book: A Memoir. He's had work in The Brownstone Poets anthologies, The Opiate, Maintenant, Sparring with Beatnik Ghosts, NYC From the Inside and The Silver-Tongued Devil anthology. Ron's papers are archived in the NYU Library.

"Jim Seegert came onto the poetry scene one evening starting at an open mic I was hosting for the Performance Poetry Association in Queens. Jim became an instant audience favorite due to his tour-de-force performances of poetry, spoken word and prose. He once started at the mic stand and formed a chain of poets dancing and chanting throughout the venue. His short stories echo that of Jack Kerouac, John Cheever and Kurt Vonnegut. He's become, over time, a literary voice whose book you will keep on your nightstand!"

James Romano
Performance Poets Association

"In Fresh Light, Jim Seegert presents a dynamic collection of pocket-sized vignettes of our pop culture. This slim but weighty volume is infused with the rhythms that formed our times—part poetry, part documentary, and a tribute to the many artists and events that helped shape the last half-century. It is presented using a seasoned storyteller's voice, a uniquely distinctive one that will speak directly to the readers of all generations."

Sal Cataldi
Contributor to NY Times, Rolling Stone, PopMatters

"I've been a fan of Jim Seegert since I first encountered his work. Reading through his collection, I'm struck anew by the qualities that first drew me to his writing—his vivid sense of place, his plain-spoken directness, and his remarkable skill as a storyteller. Because Jim, no matter what he writes—poetry, prose, memory, imagination, or his own highly individual blend of all these things—is a storyteller, and his work always has a vibrant story percolating within it. Jim's writing invites you into familiar worlds for you to see with a fresh perspective, and unfamiliar worlds that you feel like you've always known—but didn't realize it until Jim put them down on paper."

Peter Ullian, 2019-2020 City of Beacon Poet Laureate

"In Fresh Light, Jim Seegert brings the reader to face memories as though they were their own and often, as if they were happening in real time. Vivid, descriptives bring the stories and poems to life; the reader is witness to exchanges, motions and emotions, and by design, the reader becomes a part of the story."

J R Turek, Poet-In-Residence, LIP&LR, 2024-2029,
2019 LI Poet of the Year

Fresh Light

Poetry & Prose

Jim Seegert

———————————————

For Information, contact:

jrseegert@gmail.com

Print ISBN: 979-8-218-48891-8

Printed in the United States of America

First Edition

Design, production, editing, and illustration credits:

Book design and production: small packages, inc

smallpackages.com

Author Photograph: Sandy Santra ©

Front Cover Image: James Seegert ©

Back Cover Image: Sandy Santra ©

DEDICATION

To my family, my wife Liz, who edited my drafts. And to Jim Bonnett, who left us way too soon, but encourged all he touched to savor the fresh light…and pay attention to the wind chimes. RIP

Gratitude

I wish to thank the Performance Poets Association of NY for all that they have done for over a quarter century of nurturing and promoting readers throughout the NYC area. Lit/Lit in Beacon, NY and CAPs, with its global reach, for offering encouragement and a showcase for the literary arts.

I'm hesitant to put a list of names, however I must recognize:

Judy Turek and James Romano at PPA. Greg Correll, Mike Jurkovic and Jim Eve at CAPs. Michael Graves for his tireless work at the Phoenix Reading Series in NYC. To the Howland Center for providing Donna Minkowitz's Lit/Lit a literary home. To Linda Kleinbub and the Fahrenheit Open Mic crew. Randall Fields, Charles Whetstone, Dan Sandford for reading my drafts over the years. To all of you whom I have shared a stage, seat at a salon and/or coffee afterwards. And to all the random overheard conversations in diners and public venues that offered me a phrase, a word or the seeds for inspiration.

I thank you.

Contents

Foreword   1

My Résumé   5

Memories Are My Companions   7

Deep into the Ether   9

Accidental Valentine   10

Music Therapy   13

Ode to an Old City Street   17

The Library   20

Frozen in Time   22

DIY   24

Mindfulness   27

Time and Distance   29

Palace of the King   31

You Need Some Space   35

Tableaux Caught In Time   41

New Year's Day [2024]   43

Midwinter's Trip (Poet's Café) Wright Stuff   49

Last Winter Light—First World Problems   58

Spring is Coming (Tax Time)   62

On Time   65

Breath of Spring, June 2023   69

Drifting and Drifting Pt. 1   71

Drifting and Drifting Pt.2   78

Summer Reflections   86

The Park   90

Twilight   93

Cognitive Matters   96

My Heart (and Soul)   98

Temple of the Holy Word   102

The Nonsense Worshippers Highway   104

Lost and Found   107

You Have a Nice Pace   109

No One Told Us   111

December's Child   112

Addendum   118

Foreword

Welcome to Fresh Light. You are holding a collection of poetry and prose that has, by and large, been residing in my computer and is only now beginning to see the light of day. Many works have been shared at public readings, on Zoom or on writers' forums, but here they appear for the first time as an anthology in print.

I'll cover obligatory poetic subjects such as spirituality, sunset on a quiet ocean beach, (during the summer of '69), romance, Valentine's Day dinner, in a Chinese restaurant, (sorry, no wine, roses, chocolate mousse or cake), and winter in New England, (sitting by the fire on a snowy evening). We'll also visit grittier subjects like dank, smoky music dives in the industrial Midwest, Canadian wildfires, plus a few tougher realities. And we'll hit some of the required hot spots: Brooklyn, Toronto, Provincetown and the depths of my imagination.

An occasional tale may be difficult at first reading to ascertain how we got from point A to point B or exactly what the story is about—have fun—it's intended. My job is to send you down paths of myth, mirth, irony, and the occasional heartbreak, while experiencing the sweet bonds of friendship, (with a subtle touch of genteel Bohemianism tossed in). You'll emerge from these pages, entertained, engaged but totally unscathed. Not to worry!

A disclaimer will preface these tales forbidding you to share this work in every known mechanical and digital manner. And rightly so; however, if compelled to share my stories with friends or family, try this if you will, share by word of mouth. Old school. Sit down by the fire, next to the tall clock, or out on the deck in your favorite chair with the dog, a drink and a friend. Read/Talk/Engage.

Works for me.

For you?

Enjoy.

Jim Seegert

Hudson Valley, NY

July 2024

My Résumé

I need to write about myself
And where I am from?

From the frozen lakeshore—
Born in ice and snow.

Where family graves overlook
The valley below.

Where the air was acrid
And the river burned.

Where pigs are of iron
And the coke was hot.

Where music filled the air—
Classical to rock.

Where healthcare is
World class—for some.

Where Stress sang with
His harmonica.

Where the Thinker remains
Crippled by a bomb.

Where I graduated high school
And college of art.

Where I studied paint, photography
And Brautigan.

Presented in one
Hundred words—or less.

Memories Are My Companions

The past is never dead.
It's not even past.

—William Faulkner

Deep into the Ether

I dove deep

Into my ether

Past memories

Lost in time

Through synapses

Laid dormant

Passing intimate conversations

And monumental truths

Must I hold all rights

To these experiences?

Shouldn't they have

Expired over time?

Departed with those

Whose souls moved on

And rightfully reside

Somewhere near eternity—

Not sequestered

In my mind…

Accidental Valentine

Mid-February evening
We were downtown
It was getting dark
Two couples
Doing something
Who knows?
Maybe shopping
Time to eat
Hit the Dragon?
Yes! Please!

The Golden Dragon
A superb place
Authentic fare
Tablecloths, Napkins
No Formica
No take-away joint
Climb a narrow
Steep flight of stairs

Above the noisy
Crowded streets

Busy evening

Not usual

More diverse

Fewer Asians

Finally seated

Told, So sorry

A bit of a wait

On orders tonight

February 14th

We all gazed at each other—

St. Valentine's Day?

Not such a big deal

Not like in the States

Plenty of red and gold

No need to decorate

The Dragon for tonight.

Questioned ourselves...

Here is where couples

Seek to celebrate

The arrow's quivering flight?

Close by the

Windows overlooking

Dundas Street's glare

Chinatown's hustle

Filling the air

Flashes from streetcars

Rumbling slowly below

Through a gentle urban snow

Awaiting service

To begin

Grasped a noodle

Between my sticks

Dipping gently

Into sweet duck sauce

Placed it tenderly—

Upon her lips.

But I have promises to keep,
And miles to go before I sleep,
And miles to go before I sleep.

—Robert Frost

Craving some entertainment?

Need a story?

A poem?

Song?

How about—

Route 66?

Music Therapy

Once-upon-a-time…

I'd go the whole nine yards

Maybe, nine and a half,

To catch that tune

It was mid-winter

Snow, ice, deep-freeze, but

I knew where I could

Get my fix

Of Route 66

The basement

Of the club

Journey of only

A few blocks

Left the comfort of our loft

To venture out with friends

Rode the freight elevator

Down to the back dock

The rhetorical question,

What were you guys smokin'

Or thinking?

Rang true

Even before

We hoisted the gate

And exited the freight

An avalanche of arctic air

Walk?

Hell no!

No one walks

From here

To Route 66

Not tonight

Brushed off the car

Chiseled off the ice

Got her started—
Drove
Those few blocks
To the warmth
Of the club

Dim light
Blue smoky haze
Rhythm of the band
They were already drunk
(We were, only halfway there)

Could have hunkered down
Back home
Killed-off the Bombay
And Tanqueray
But no—
No—not this night
Needed some R'n'R
Some drivin' music
Some high octane
Some kicks
The wide-open road
The wind in our hair

The desert SW

Flagstaff, Arizona

California—

(Forget Chicago)

More than 2,000 miles

Of wailing harmonica

Pounding riffs

Flying high

On *66*

I got *my* kicks

My way

On the highway…

That's the best!

<blockquote>
I was stunned and amazed
My childhood memories
Slowly swirled past
Like the wind through the trees
—Christine Hynde, "My City was Gone"
</blockquote>

Ode to an Old City Street

I searched for you online last night,

Seeking images of our past.

So many things have vanished

But you're still there alas.

You're:

Old enough to remember

Horses' hooves and

Wagons

Old enough to remember

When you were paved

With brick

Old enough to remember

The street car and

Church bells

Old enough to remember
The library
And school

Old enough to remember
Trees shading you
From sun

Old enough to remember
My relatives
My birth

Old enough to remember
My tiny soft
Footsteps

Old enough to remember
The hard times and
The good

Old enough to remember
No vacant lots
With trash

Old enough to *understand*
The fickle hand
Of fate

Old enough to *realize*
Your days might be
Numbered

Old enough to *recognize*
Looming urban
Thunder

My stoic veteran of
These shifting winds
Of time—

I loved you many years ago…

Do you remember me?

Henritize.

The Library

I remember how the books smelled
Different from anything else
I can see in my mind the children's section
To the right, in the back
And reminded only to whisper
It was eerily quiet

I carefully chose which books to borrow
They had hard, thick covers
They were heavy
Some wrapped in plastic
I could only choose
So many

I remember a large machine at checkout
It made a loud Ka-thunk
Cards were slipped into pockets
On the back covers
Stamped with dates
Smelling of ink

I can picture my grandmother
Clutching her library card
I can still feel the mammoth rooms
With tall windows full of light
In the Carnegie Library
On the corner of her block

They are both long gone now
Those windows all bricked over
I can imagine Andrew Carnegie
And Grandma,
Gyrating—
In their graves

Frozen in Time

Two vintage leather sleigh bell reins
Hung near the doorway of the shop
Stretching from the low ceiling to just above the floor.

These were my father's, he said, giving them a slight jingle.
He was a teamster—had a dozen horses in the day.
They were a lot of work.
Feeding them on a cold winter's night in a stable lit by
       ¬ gas lanterns.
Tossing hay down from the loft above.

They still smell a bit like leather, I said.
I know, he replied.

You came here to use the table saw.
She has a new blade.
Will cut this clear white pine like butter, he said,
While inspecting my lumber.
You need the rail?

Yes, I have to run bevels.
And I'll need the miter as well.

You can angle the blade down here on this end for your rips.
The T is hanging below on your right.
Push your sticks through with this.

Finally he handed me a well-worn tape measure off his
        ¬ workbench.
And pulled a sharpened pencil out of an ancient coffee can.

That should do it, he said.
Measure 'em twice, cut 'em once.
Let 'er rip.

It's been close to fifty years since I visited the shop.
Borrowing the saw—to cut a stretcher frame on a snowy
        ¬ evening.
I must have misplaced half a century of memories during
        ¬ that time,
But not that of the aging craftsman, his kindness…
Nor the bells.

DIY

For some reason I was tasked/decided to

Paint the kitchen in my home.

Room needed a paint job, it could be argued.

Decorative motifs from former owners

Were still adorning the place.

Nails and screws protruded from the walls for no

 apparent reason

And the exterior door exhibited a maturing yellow white.

I met Angel at the paint shop.

He fortunately had the time to help me select what I needed.

We talked primers

And he also suggested a Kitchen/Bathroom formulation of

wall paint in the same brand that I was contemplating.

Mold and mildew resistant. Same price range. Not cheap.

I trudged home with most of the needed supplies

But not everything, of course,

And set to work.

It took me a day to tape around the wooden cabinets with

their complex crown moldings, patch the minor holes and

the much larger ones hidden by some of the afore men-

tioned decorative embellishments.

I primed over the walls with two coats of a time-honored primer, paying extra attention to the corners and the patched holes.

I aggravated an old, reoccurring back injury and took some time off one morning to visit the gym. If one visits the gym for R and R and a breath of fresh air, one must be in shoddy shape. Time well spent I thought,

As I let paint dry between coats during days of record humidity and rainfall.

Back was better, for a day.

I rolled the topcoats on and then revisited the paint shop for trim paint—something for the door, interior and out, and for use on the baseboards as well. I was looking for an off white…maybe semi-gloss…maybe a satin.

Andrew, an old timer (as if I should speak), the paint shop manager, was holding the fort. I explained what I needed and received seasoned advice as I explained colors I was contemplating. Some of the color sample strips were out of stock and I settled upon a hue that I had selected at home out of a catalogue but it now seemed to have a new name (but same mix code).

This happens, I was told. Marketing.

Can you mix this in a semi-gloss, I asked.

Soft Gloss, he replied…

What's that?

Same thing, he said.

I thanked him, took it home and discovered the mix was a bit brighter than I expected but suitable.

I have a degree in painting and worked for decades in the graphic arts business…

I find the vagaries of precision in this kind of color work vexing at times.

I peeled the tape off the cabinets, floors and door glass, touched things up a bit, cleaned up the mess and called it a week.

However, I still don't know if I really needed to do all this shit.

Or, was I—

Just dancing around.

Mindfulness

One should wake with mindfulness I'm told…begin each day finding the focus of your thoughts before one's feet hit the floor. Breathe deeply, ease into each day.

I awoke this morning to a stuffy-headed mind full of music and intense imagery. Alannah Myles singing Black Velvet at the 1999 Montreux Jazz Festival.

I was focused.

I could hear the drums, a methodical repetitious beat reminiscent of Moe Tucker in the Velvets. Plus a powerful bass line, one of my all time weaknesses, or strengths. And Alannah's sultry rock and roll style, melodic yet uber-gutsy. Not like most of the Canadian performers exported to the US. We have a softer more folksy image of Canadians; Joni Mitchel, Gordon Lightfoot, Leonard Cohen, even Neil Young, all very popular but not cruising the stage in Switzerland batting over a mic stand while belting out an ode to an American rock legend—in heels.

I'm feeling more mindful, good enough to arise and make

some coffee. I'm interrupted during this part of my estab-lished morning ritual by two Granddaughters who didn't want a kiss, but wished to perform a song instead.

A duet.
Face-to-face.

Singing/Shouting:

Na-nah Nanah, Poo Poo
Na-nah Nanah, Poo Poo
Na-nah Nanah, Poo Poo

Strong/Melodic/Gutsy

I'm unsure if this was an original or a cover

I didn't record it
For posterity
For some morning
For some mindfulness
I did write it down though…

My day begins.

The distinction between the past, present and future
Is only a stubbornly persistent illusion.

—*Albert Einstein*

Time and Distance

I live close to the beginning of time

I used to live much further but now I live closer

How close?

Practically around the corner

In Dutchess County

North of where the Appalachian Trail crosses I-84

In New York is an exposed section of rock—

Precambrian Grenville

North American bedrock, coughed-up

On old Stormville Mt.

It's hard to miss, there's a survey marker nearby

1.1 to 1.3 billion years old

They say.

That's plus or minus a couple hundred million years

It cooked for a while

You may find it in other places

Scandinavia to Antarctica

Possibly Australia

It got around

Back in the day

I first touched this timeless rock along the Trail

Over 20 years ago

It's also in Ontario

I lived there

Eons ago

In Toronto timeless rock could be found

Along Spadina Ave. just south of College

43.657477° N, 79.400146° W

At the el Mocambo club

I felt rock at the elMo 50 years ago

Everyone rocked there

Even the Stones

The club hasn't moved

I have

I got around

Back in the day

Some say I should be

More focused on the present

The 21st Century

The here and now!

Bury memories from the past

Remember: take-out-the-garbage-tonight.

That's in the future

I'll travel down that road in due time

I'm writing at present

Yeah, I could spend a
A month of Sundays
Talkin' 'bout the places
I've been.
      —*Freddy King*

Palace of the King

Can't get Freddie King's

Palace of the King

Outta my head today…

Used to travel cross-town

To hear Stress

Belt out that tune at

The Euclid Tavern

116th and Euclid

Edge City

Cleveland

Late 70's

The Euc

An urban relic

Dive incarnate

Dark

Smoky

Cheap bottled beer

Bare wood floors

Maybe a small cover
Maybe not
Warm in the winter
An *oven* in the summer
Ventilation?
Open the back door
Step outside
Old school.

Mr. Stress Blues Band
Took the stage
Saturdays
Friday, Stress said,
Was date night
Saturdays you come
To hear the music.
The guys and him
Doc on keyboards
Was, well, a doc.
Day jobs disappeared
For everyone…
On Saturday nights
At the Tavern

Stress took

Some liberties on Palace

Personalized it a bit

I bet King would have

Been OK with it—

I've played in London

Tokyo

California

Now fuckin' O-hi-o

I'm just a short

Little fat man

*Who sings the Blues…**

Playing harp/singing

While smoking

His soft gravely voice

Rising from a battered soul

I've been 'round the world

I've heard many things

Nothing can make me satisfied

*But these Blues I sing…***

Tryin' to make it real—

Compared to What?

On those dark smoky

Saturday nights…

You could feel it

We all felt it

Livin'…in the palace…of the king. **

RIP

*   *Mr. Stress (William (Bill) Miller)*

** *Freddy King (Frederick Christian), Palace of the King*

You Need Some Space

Tropical birds fluttered throughout the kitchen as you studied tins and jars of globally-sourced exotic loose teas on a shelf above the counter, next to the window. Among tea balls, stirrers and assorted jars of honey, you were surprised to discover a stack of round Typhoo bags. *Tastefully diverse,* you thought.

Your thoughts were interrupted when serenely gliding into the room through a beaded curtain, apparently wearing only scarves, an orchid in her long auburn hair and a transparent veil of Patchouli, she entered, the consummate embodiment of The Breath of Spring.

"Welcome…extending her hand…I'm Djuna. My apologies if I'm late, I was in the shower. Your key worked OK, I see."

"Yes."

"My brother is at his day job—you manage his band, right?"

"And play rhythm guitar," you stated.

She proceeded to fill a kettle with water at the sink, lit her gas stove with a long wooden match and filled a well-used tea ball with organic Jasmine. All in a fluid flowing motion as if done a million times.

"While the kettle is heating I'd like to show you the space downstairs where Joe practices. I'm hopeful that you will find it suitable for storing the group's gear."

"Sure, that's why I'm here."

Opening a cupboard door, she removed a key dangling from a nail, slipped into sandals and unlocked a steel fire door adjoining the kitchen. She led the way for you down a flight of industrial metal stairs into the basement.

It was a relatively open space with peeling white brick walls, yellowing acoustic tiles on the ceiling and a floor covered with some God-awful dark green multi colored broken vinyl squares from the 1950s. It felt dry. Joe had his complete drum kit set up along the far wall, cymbals shimmering in the filtered incandescent light. It was also obvious that you'd share this space with Djuna's studio, which was partitioned off by a large black curtain. Of note were moveable lights, extension cords, a working fridge, bathroom and a couple turntables. All good signs. This area may have been used as living space at one time. It definitely lacked the skylight, airiness, plants and the convenience of a freight elevator as did your loft...but it would do. And the space seemed secure.

A tomb of sorts, the basement harbored an aromatic blend of raw canvass, paint, hash and sage. *Perfect...feels like home,* you thought. No cats.

"Joe said maybe we could to do some run-throughs and practices here in addition to using the space for storage," you mentioned to the proprietress.

"That's groovy...noise is no issue...he practices drums down here." [*But* not *bass guitar,* you thought.] The kettle began whistling from above.

Djuna carefully led you by hand upstairs, offering you a chair at the small round table in her kitchen.

Scarves twirling, she poured steaming water into an elegant ceramic English teapot, careful not to spill a drop.

"Well?" she said as she placed the lid on the pot.

"I think the space will work out fine…if you don't mind four or five guys hauling stuff right through your kitchen at all hours of the day and very early morning."

"Ooooh, a parade of young men—musicians—coming through my place day and night—ummm how won-der-ful. But *unfortunately*, I'll be away for several months starting next week. Joe helps me out with the rent so that's not a problem and not a burden for you guys, but the band *will* split the utilities with me."

Not a question.

"That's the deal…and no parties."

"Sure." (It's a steal).

She poured tea into two mismatched ornately glazed blue cups. You sat in silence savoring the fragrant brew. She then coolly drifted over to where you were sitting.

You took another sip.

She effortlessly slid onto your lap.

She is *only wearing scarves,* you thought.

Ummm.

Ummm.

Whispering, "Let me take these off *first,*" she sensuously re-moved…your glasses.

Then, while delighting in delicately whisking your face with her soft fragrant tresses, inquired discretely, "Where would you like my first kiss?"

"I'd love to seal this deal."

A Parakeet alighting on the table squawked, *Jaz—min Jaz—min.*

A Parrot, *En—joy…En—joy…En—joy.*

Tableaux Caught In Time

New Year's Day [2024]

I don't travel much on holidays

Anymore.

Used to all the time

Between Thanksgiving—New Year's Day.

All the time.

Many family birthdays

During this period as well.

Including mine.

Toronto, Michigan, Cleveland.

Weather too bad to fly—

Drive the Volvo.

Follow the semi tracks in the snow

Until they slip off

The road.

Spent a birthday once

In Martinique.

Not applicable for this yarn.

It's been very mild season

This year.

Scary nice.

My elderly friend in New England

Stayed home

On New Year's as well
His family was in Florida
Sick of airline hassles,
Obnoxious travelers,
Annoying relatives,
Bogus weather.
Home alone.
Peace.

Thought maybe
I should pay him a visit
Drive up for the day
Visit Father Time himself
Kick out the old
Ring in the new

I don't drink anymore
Hard to believe
I'm no fun
6-8 gin and tonics
No more
6-8 seltzers on the rocks
With lime
Not before driving

Come on up

I'll make a real dinner.

Hit the highway

40's, light drizzle

Why hadn't it been like this

Years ago?

Father Time greeted me at the door

Easy ride?

Smooth

Bring some poetry?

Yep.

I'm working on some haiku

Maybe you'll listen later…

He said.

Sure, I'm game.

Took a seat by the fire

Place smells great

What's on the menu?

Sole Almondine

Roasted asparagus

Stewed eggplant

Cranberry butternut soup

For starters

Ok?
Sure.
And some bubbly—
San Pellegrino water
That goes with this French fare?
Mediterranean
Right.

Wonderful venue
Delicious food
Polite staff
Private table
Courteous clientele
Crackling fire
No tab/No tip
Free parking

Let's kick off the New Year
With a toast
For auld lang syne my friend
For auld lang syne
No debating
Robert Burns
Scottish translations
Or such

Clink

Take a cup of kindness
Enjoy
Edvard Grieg, Keith Jarrett
Dylan and scented candles
Filled the air this night
Before leaving the table
A cordial was offered,
In lieu of his aged Port,
One of my host's
Poems
Specifically written for
The occasion:

Sumatra Dark Roast
Ethiopian Heirloom
Earl Grey tonight?

What do you think?
Oh, It's all-good
I'll have whatever
You're thinking
Any of the trinity

Upon completing dinner
I reestablished my position
Sitting down by the fire
Next to the tall clock
Staring into the flickering flames
Of an impending New Year

My thoughts, however,
Were drawn to—
An unnamed Italian poet
(From the 13th century),*
Vintage aged Port
And Rosemary

But never to…
The Jack of Hearts

*Bob Dylan, Tangled up in Blue

Midwinter's Trip (Poet's Café) Wright Stuff

I promised a friend on New Year's Day I'd come up to visit
sometime over the course of the winter.

Today appears to be a good time—sunny mid-winter
morning, mild weather.
Good-to-go.

My family wants me to visit him more often. This request
is from those disinterested in doing the same. They're
looking for me to supply some kind of report on the old
man's situation, which they then question. Those that do
the least complain the most. Always.
I look forward to these visits. We discuss poetry or art or
music or food, occasionally politics. He also exemplifies
congeniality at its finest, in my opinion.

I occupy my solitude on the road by listening, uninter-
rupted, to playlists on my phone. Bliss. Leonard Cohen is
up today…I repeat many songs.

This visit was prefaced as an invitation to spend the day
at the *Poet's Café*. He's probably already mulled over a
stack of books, from his extensive personal library, as

fuel for discussion. He's mindful that I'm not a classicist nor drawn to work from much over a century ago. His interest stems from a studious deep dive into an old hobby.
Gotta love it.

Upon arriving, I mentioned how mild the winter had been, so far. *Commenting on winter weather around here is always an icebreaker,* he says.

A line he's used, well, a million times…

We set right to work, drinking tea in his sun-filled kitchen, exchanging pleasantries about friends, family, how the ride was and my car's demeanor, while seated at a table cluttered with books. He sparked my interest immediately, by mentioning that he's been studying the complete works of James Wright, aware that I have been reading him since high school.

Great, what did you discover?

Hook, he said.
Know it?

Yes!

Not his most well known, nor really his style in my opinion, but a masterpiece. With a significant moral at the end.

How so?

Accept gifts; whatever they may be, when sincerely offered.

Yep, my take as well.

It reminds me of when my son and I shoveled the stairs and sidewalks for the frail elderly lady next door and she wanted to give us some cash but we said, No thanks. Hours later she trudged over, knocked on our door delivering fresh baked cookies and brownies. We kind of originally dissed her, I think, by not accepting her cash offering (which she un-doubtedly considered it to be). She only wished to show us her gratitude. It's tricky.

I took it
It wasn't the money I needed.
*But I took it. **

So, does *Hook* refer to the one-handed character, who one-ups Wright unintentionally over their shared miseries, or the close?

Both.

Scholars will be dismissing us as not seeing the cosmos, heaven and earth or Oedipus, Ulysses and Jesus, or something…

Tell them, Thank you.
It's not the irony we needed.
But we'll take it.

What's in this tea by the way?

Honey. Just drink it up.

We went on for a couple hours appraising Wright's work. Hitting upon several of my all-time favorites including: *In Response to a Rumor That the Oldest Whorehouse in Wheeling, West Virginia Has Been Condemned.*
This poem demanded significant attention. I don't recall how the poem was dissected in my English class but we agreed it too ends with a hook at the end.
As in the meaning of the word used earlier. Not sure that we were even searching for a common thread…

We eventually landed upon:

Autumn Begins in Martin's Ferry, Ohio: Not politically correct
in these times, I suppose. People of Polish ancestry are now
usually referred to as Poles. African Americans…well he
could have done much worse. Writing in common conversa-
tional vernacular doesn't always age well. You dig?
Strong, concise and with a bit of a twist in the title, It's still
popular. The story line hasn't changed in over half a
century. That was easily agreed upon. Agreeing on the con-
cept of correctness was totally another matter though.

Break for a bit of late lunch?

Sure.

The kitchen, since I arrived, had been bathed in the aroma
of soup slowly simmering on the stove. Cannellini, oregano,
shallots, with a hint of basil, my guess.

Tuscan bean, I was informed.
It was more-like the consistency of a rich vegetable stew along
with fresh spinach added before serving for good measure.
Accompanied by a platter of deli, fruits and cheeses—Shaved

Parmesan Romano, Balsamic glazed Mozzarella,
and Cheddar.

Cheddar? I asked politely.

*This isn't Tuscany. The cheddar is local—aged, very sharp and
quite edible. Enjoy.*

Well, look who's here! Does he need to go out?

*He's not going anywhere. Not as long as cheese is on the table. He's
taken to sleeping all day until the fridge door opens…Pardon me, I
should take this call.*

Buddy loved the cheese. We're forever pals now. The meats
except for some turkey were pretty much off-limits for a dog
though. Garlic and such. Upon ending his call, I was offered
another bowl and politely questioned whether I had fed any
soup to the dog.

There's onion in it and also I have to live with him after eating beans.

No. No—he's *clean,* I vowed.
The call was from a friend in town whom he promised to

see tomorrow but due to forecasted overnight snow suggest-
ed he cancel. She's not well, he said.

So, look, I don't have to linger much longer. I know there's a
standing invitation to spend the night but perhaps I should
consider hitting the trail before it gets too late and the
weather changes. You could run over later this evening?

That would be very considerate. But, did we wrap-up Wright?
He questioned.

Never.

Never.

*I'll prepare you some solid fuel and fresh brewed French Roast
for your ride. Meanwhile take a look at this,* as he rummaged
through his kitchen collection bemoaning the demise of
independent bookstores. Something new.

The Bookstore Book, by Ron Kolm.

Wonderful memoir chronicling a lifetime spent in the Life in NYC.

Thanks, I shouted, over the whirling coffee grinder. I got

possibly a third of the way through, while sampling the coffee, up to, *Ugly George,* as our day drew to a close.

Take it with you, finish it but please, bring it back.

I'm no biblioklept.

I wouldn't have offered if you were, he laughed.
What are you going to tell them about me this time?

Oh, that you're fine, sustaining yourself nicely on…poetry and bean soup.

Excellent! Excellent!
What about the cane?

Well, actually, I've never thought to mention it…

Thank you.
Here, enjoy and please don't stop at any roadside attractions to eat.

Thanks. Till next time.

Next time. Drive safely my friend. Ciao.

Ciao.

I started the car, placing my buffet on the passenger seat before leaving. Damn! He stuck a fifty in there with a note apologizing that he didn't have, *any nourishment for the car.*

I turned the engine off and was about to go back in when I noticed him standing by the kitchen window…He smiled and waved.

I took it
It wasn't the money I needed.
*But I took it. ***

** Hook, James Wright*

Last Winter Light—First World Problems

The room was growing darker as the last vestiges of a late winter day's achromatic light seeped through the leaded glass windows of the den. Rising from the chair you throw several pieces of well-seasoned split white ash along with a prized piece of Osage orange onto the hearth, quickly closing the glass doors. *That should hold us for most of the night,* you said. [Though it wasn't clear if that statement was directed towards me, or the hourglass urn upon the mantle.]

A cup of English tea is steaming on a lone stone coaster resting upon an antique cedar chest, facing the chair where you will spend a good deal of the evening. The dark, well-oiled, cedar glistens in the flickering light of the fire. While flashing lights and the rumble of a passing plow on the lane just beyond the low stone wall gives you a sense of assurance that all is being taken care of and not to worry.

But as you carefully choose whether to swirl a spoonful of bourbon honey or lemon honey into your tea, you pause to ponder your situation. Could the tranquility of your well-ordered life possibly be only an intensifying state of melancholy? Are you actually *living* on the time-honored family estate, or merely a caretaker of a piece of aging real estate from a bygone era? First world problems, you reason, attempting to dismiss your predicament.

You take a long slow sip of your tea. Your eyes survey the room: from the bookcases, to the piano, to the globe, past the Miró, settling on the Kandinsky print your father purchased in Switzerland.

A museum of sorts, you suppose.

You told me that your sister had asked you multiple times to come to Florida and live the easy life. *Easy for her,* you scoffed. *She's living off her inheritance, plus her half of the estate that that I bought and matrimony—enough to afford a pricey high-rise condo on the beach and expensive German automobiles.* Not exactly a generator of wealth for herself or her community, as is your family's tradition. Besides, kvetching beside the pool, playing cards or snorting cocaine aren't activities that you hold dear. Not insignificantly, you always remind her that there aren't any alligators in New England. And as the steward of the family's local philanthropies, shouldn't you have an obligation to reside locally? Excellent excuses.

Excellent.

Additionally, whether he appreciates it or not, your son relies on your frequent counsel in administering what is left of the family business. *He's hanging on to what hasn't evaporated,* you lament. Your primary enterprise recently, however, has been trying to come to terms with what is actually present-day western business evolution and what appears increasingly to be a unique American de-evolution. Devo. You could lecture a graduate course on this subject, but feel powerless to do anything about it.

You eventually reach for the remote resting beside you to catch the local evening news—brilliantly washing the den with the LED flat screen's electronic glow. The program opens with a tease about the weather, a Hollywood celebrity scandal and news of new dysfunction within the federal government. Then segues into an advertisement for a Swedish car, much like yours, tearing through pristine snowdrifts—in a fashion that none who actually purchased a car like this would ever actually do.

You hit the mute.

You soon switch to an international cable news station and glance at the crawl.

The Russians did what?

You quickly punch unmute.

A chill shoots down your spine. Befitting a gentleman of habitual reserve, you take another sip of tea and during this moment of totally restrained silence discreetly ask your-self…What–the–fuck?

Spring is Coming (Tax Time)

You rise from the kitchen table to get another cup of coffee, stopping by the window to peer out through the mist at the soft light emanating from the carriage house.

It's almost 6:30; Rosa and her daughter have fed the horses and will turn them out shortly. You'll need to get moving though; you have a 9:00 at the office. You are never late…and always prepared. You gaze out upon the back of the estate seriously contemplating what to do with the guys. Horses have been on the ancestral property since the earliest days; indeed, initially they were the only mode of transportation and the carriage house actually housed carriages. Well not this one, the original burned down in the early 1900's, recalling your grandfather's stories. The current one was renovated in the 1950s and thoroughly modernized some thirty years ago to better accommodate the family's stable of automobiles as well as animals. Just recently it was upgraded to the requirements of whatever the local *horse house codes* are, as you are fond of saying.

Your accountant has recommended boarding the boys to save yourself the expenses and trouble of caring for animals that you seldom ride anymore. The *Equestrian Equation* he called it as he showed you numbers—they made some sense. That's his job. He's always done well for the family. [*Wait till the new fencing invoices are added to his formulation…* you think.]

The animals are part of the family's culture. You lovingly recall riding Ted-1 as a young child and there've been a succession of Ted namesakes ever since. Yaz, probably your father's favorite, arrived when you were in college. He sired a foal that you named Carl—still in the stable. You've recently added Gronk to draw the wagon and the sleigh and apparently to tug a delivery truck out of the ditch along the lane one evening. The dog considers them his flock and alerts you to the slightest abnormalities with his charges… and they consider him their pet. They run together, in serious bliss, through the back pasture everyday. Well, not so much recently in Ted's case. You assume there must be some kind of dreadful dollar amount that can be professionally assigned to all that joyous frolicking. You'll surely be informed before the end of the month. At least they weren't written off as 21st Century Pasture Ornaments!

Life-long friends at the Club have recommended a near-by equestrian center that they personally use for boarding and rehab featuring: individual turnouts, hot and cold wash stalls, a cross country course and an excellent 24/7 staff that also provides geriatric horse care. You pause, taking a long slow sip, as Ted hobbles out.

A nursing facility for the boys—how well did that work for Mom? Noting that she and your daughter were the last members of the family to actively spend time riding the horses.
You glance at the kitchen clock, hurry to the den to retrieve your phone from its charger then grab your coat and keys from the back foyer. While placing the cell in your pocket you notice a message from your financial advisor:
Out of caution, let's review your discretionary investment advisement agreements regarding an Asian traded equity, at your earliest.

You abruptly stop as you are leaving; give the dog a quick rub behind his ears, check yourself in the mirror, grab the bag with your heels and head out—carrying a handful of carrots.

You effortlessly deal with your firm's corporate financial strategies and legal obligations but these personal issues you always find enormously—

Taxing.

On Time

You study the late day sun illuminating your office at the end of normal business hours. Your desk faces a wall of classic analogue clocks displaying time from around the world. Beneath them, plaques designating time zones and ports of call that are important to your business. The clocks were added during office renovations several years ago with the intent to replace your antique grandfather clock. The designer deemed these devices would be impressive both as a strong decorative feature and functional modernization. You've been in this business long enough, however, that you intuitively understand exactly what time (and what day) it is at the Port of Rotterdam or the Shanghai Container Facility, when it's 6:10 P.M. in your office, as it is presently. And long past are the days when anyone would think twice about contacting you at an inconvenient day or time.

Or vice-versa.

The tall clock still stands in the corner it has occupied for decades, the light of late day now warming the dark black cherry finials on the crown of the cabinet and reflecting off the pendulum, sending a glimmer of sunlight dancing around the room. Occasionally, the sun's rays strike the beveled glass door at an angle that generates a dramatic rainbow. The clock's face has always been an indicator not only of the time of day but also the phases of the moon, resplendent with a truly otherworldly, grinning, man-in-the-moon—synchronized to the days of the month. Mr. Moon would be a worthy addition to any psychedelic light show in your opinion.

And you are showing your age.

The clock strikes with deep, slow, Westminster chimes on the quarter hour, or the half as you have it set. After thoroughly terrorizing a cleaning staffer late one evening, you reset the clock not to chime or strike the hour between 7 PM and 7 AM. All's well however. The young lady's supervisor tactfully reassigned her evening duties to another part of the building—far removed from the Tick-Tock Clock.

On a wall near the clock is a small oil painting of unknown provenance. It is a dramatic depiction of a generic American clipper ship, possibly inspired by a J.O. Curtis design from

Medford, Massachusetts during the 1850s. Not a detailed rendering like the portraits of your family's vessels—possibly a romanticized artist's rendition of how a finished ship might look for a potential buyer. It's magnificent though. Her gleaming white hull coursing through the seas under a brilliant cerulean sky with the hint of oncoming sundown tinting a thin scattering of high clouds. You have always sensed that the sails may not be set *exactly* right…but man anyone worth their salt can smell the sea from across the room.

It was skillfully varnished and has been well preserved, barely yellowing or cracking. The painting carries a strange poetic inscription inscribed on a metal plate attached to the frame dated 1855…

…the huge-hulled clean shaped New-York clipper at sea under steam or full sail gleams with unmatched beauty…[1]

Your cell phone alarm vibrates.

It's time to leave for the Art Museum's annual spring Fund Raising Gala! You relish socializing at the cocktail hour before the dinner and have been looking forward to attending, as you do every year. Your pockets may not be as deep as they once were, but your philanthropic gift is always offered and appreciated as just that—a true gift. No strings.

You pat your jacket pocket to check for your wallet, keys and check the phone…

You have a new message:

It's Diane…from the office…in Rotterdam.

What could she want? It's after 11 P.M. there…

Sir, may I have just a minute…of your time?

** Leaves of Grass, Walt Whitman 1855*

Breath of Spring, June 2023

I'll speak of—

No daffodils in the dew.

No robins in the park.

No butterflies on the wing.

Nothing like that—nothing.

Under an oxide blanket of a retro 20th century-style rust belt

sky, I sit in self-quarantine. The air quality index unhealthy

and rising. An air purifier plugged in by my side as the AC

hums during this cool/dry late spring day.

Will this be the new normal?

I drift off to sleep with random, scattered, stuffy-headed,

dreams of past summers bouncing in my brain.

Memories of Cape Cod National Seashore and Truro Light

buffeted by fresh breezes floating off the Atlantic. Followed

by a day trip while on the opposite coast to the aromatic soft

forest floor of Muir Woods. Nice. Tranquil. Refreshing.

A decision, made after several slices and a couple beers at

the end of a long day to drive from San Francisco to Boulder,

CO by dinner the next night, the ethers of leaded-gasoline

exhaust in the thin high desert night air fueling my joyride.

Then a thrilling cruise on the Cross Bronx Expressway after camping in the Catskills.

The diesel exhaust of a ferry crossing the Bay of Fundy on a beautiful calm day. Clouds of cigarette smoke curling through a murky blues dive in the industrial Midwest.

I float down into the National Air Shows, serene out on the Toronto Islands but smoky, gritty and *loud* in Cleveland, standing on the sweltering tarmac or along the freight car rails, so fitting for that town. I'm in a plume of castor oil smoke from a vintage Sopwith Camel at the Old Rhinebeck Aerodrome, then the full stench of LaGuardia Airport upon arrival home after a summer sojourn.

A cough jolts me out of this brain fog or maybe the notification on my phone, warning that the air quality from Canadian wild fires has gotten worse—I should remain indoors, if at all possible.

I'm in. It stinks! I fish for my handkerchief. I spit up some phlegm.

Right now, I'd swap all those airy memories for one *precious* June experience: That long slow-dance in Montreal underneath a crystal-clear sky with the stars sparkling above—[starry, starry night.]

I must be dreaming…

Drifting and Drifting Pt. 1

You stir in your chair. Your playlist is "Jim's Favorite '60's Classics." A cool early summer breeze flutters the blinds as it wafts through the open windows of the den. You've been asleep for some time…and you've drifted, drifted back into August 1969 with Jim standing on deck filming the approach, navigating past twin jetties. An afternoon mist accompanied by soft rain shrouds you as you glide towards the distant harbor…*I'm driftin' and driftin' like a ship out on the sea…Nobody seems to want me…Except the wide and open sea*[1].

On cue, the sun dramatically bursts through the growling dark clouds to the southwest…the harbor fades up into full view bathed in Peter Max-like sunbeams. Complete with gulls fluttering through the panorama as Nantucket town comes closer into view. You're passing Brant Light to starboard, clean, brisk wind buffeting your hair, sea spray in your face, the strap of your boonie hat slipped around your neck. You have come in peace, to drop out for a while…to drop out for a while.

A flotilla of pleasure craft from far and wide fills the harbor;
a magnificent tall ship from London flying the Union Jack,
a power cruiser from Kingston, with the new Jamaican flag,
Halifax, Boston, Hyannis. Lots of sails. You picture yourself...
On a great big clipper ship going from this land here to that...[2]

But actually, you've come here to drop out for a while.

Once ashore, you marvel at how much effort has been taken
to preserve the 19th century town. A cool breeze caresses
you. You rent bicycles, receiving detailed instructions and
a tourist map on how to get across the Island to Surfside—
where to avoid the really *wicked* cobblestone streets. You're
hungry...you get a tip where to eat. Sitting outside on a porch
you remember ordering burgers, fries, an iced tea, a frappe, a
couple spumoni ice creams. Life passes you by on the street.
The waitress says she is very busy and excuses herself for the
slow service. You don't care. You're savoring the fresh light.
She thinks you guys are being exceptionally polite.

You have come here to drop out...for a while.

The waitress is busy...*one girl quit today to go back to school.*
Two of her friends left the Island to attend an outdoor music

fair somewhere in New York. She's staying one more week; she needs the money for college—Amherst. You guys are good with school to after Labor Day you say. Groovy, she says. It's mid-August 1969. Yesterday's paper from Boston sits on the next table. You see Ted Kennedy's picture with a map of neighboring Chappaquiddick Island. You're not interested in today's Massachusetts's news spin. You have come here to drop out for a while. And pay attention to the wind chimes.

You walk your bikes up from harbor-side, seeking Pleasant Street. The sweet scent of patchouli and soft strains of Donovan float through the screen door of a head shop. You stop to read a sign displayed in front of an elegant lodging establishment listing rooms without phones, as one of its many posh amenities. Jim mentions something about this being the right *attitude*. You trek uphill off the cobbles. It's only a couple miles once you leave town to Surfside on the south side of the island. Your touristy rental bikes took some getting used to. There wasn't a big selection…you could tell. They had nifty woven and wire baskets on the handlebars. Good for a bathing suit and a towel. With seats that tortured your tush—and gears to match.
You have come here to drop out for a while.

Surfside is the end of the road, literally. You've reached your goal, the Youth Hostel—right on the beach. Managed by what may have been a young mom and pop team (teachers?). It is situated where people with all the means in the universe would want to be…and where those folks would never ever stay. Perfect. You check in. There is a long list of rules, which seem to make sense, about cooking, sanitation, food storage, noise, smoking…rolling papers, cheap wine, flatulence and bad karma as you recall.
A small rustic store is located close to the hostel, offering enough fare to get by.

You have come here to drop out for a while.

The fog rolls in.

The teen group that comprises the primary residents of this bunkhouse today are members of a bicycling summer camp that flew from the east coast to Frisco, peddled across a good chunk of the continent, had a week to kill and is spending a couple days on the Island and The Vineyard for R and R. They just rolled in from a 50-mile circumnavigation of the Island. Pumped. It should be noted in your memory that your mother never bought you a Peugeot touring bike in Greenwich Village to get rid of you for the entire summer. But, it soon became obvious why one would. You shared little interest in the nuances of derailleurs; tire types, or whom one may have for their 10th grade teachers, nor endlessly repeated tales and adventures of pubic hair…wherever it may be located. You have come here to drop out for a while.

You stir in your chair considering waking from this dream. Intrepidly, you sail forth…

Sunshine came softly a-through my a-window today…[3]
…The morning brings sun pouring through the windows of the dormitory style room, the fresh smell of the ocean through the porch door and an ice cold shower.
You spend the day bicycling across the Island in the hot, shade-less August sun returning to cook dinner and eat outside on the weathered wooden picnic tables. Everything on the Island outside of town seems to be unpainted weathered wood—an aesthetic code. Garnished with soft sand and flowers.

Your hosts inform you that it's their after dinner thing to head down to the beach and watch the sunset…they invite you to hang with them. Several of the adult leaders from the trans-continental bikers join in. This custom of your hosts, on pleasant evenings, normally includes a bottle or two of Mateus, sand, surf, sky, the ocean and the sun. There really isn't anything else to do here at night you are told. *There's a movie theater in town, if you want. The Hostel doesn't have a TV. This is what we do.* That's OK.

You have come here to drop out for a while.

You guys arrive empty handed but that's cool, you are impromptu guests. You are both totally awestruck by the unspoiled beauty of the beach and marvel at how peaceful it is. Jim wanders into the surf. No one comes here much at this time we are told. It's ours tonight…no tourists, no locals, no fires. No smoking, please. Several long sticks of Tibetan sandalwood are lit and placed securely in the sand. Sitting in a circle passing the bottle it is immediately noted that the days are getting shorter. The summer is fading. The 1960s are almost gone. *What's your take? Where are you from? Where are you going? What brought you here? Are you guys brothers? What happened to the Kennedys? Brian Jones? Genteel bohemian-ism? The Mets?* No one mentions the war?
We have come here to drop out for a while.

A hand full of sand is sifting slowly between fingers of a young woman's hand…*We are like these grains of sand scattered in the wind. We are stardust. We are cosmic. We walked on the Moon! Far out, man. Far Out.* As the sun begins to drop behind the horizon silence envelopes our circle. The moon, the stars, the setting sun, the call of a lone gull…the timeless lap of the surf. Our primeval womb. Peace…and Peace again…Peace.

We have come here to drop out for a while.

Arrived.

Drifting and Drifting Pt.2

By the time you rolled into Provincetown your self-imposed island isolation was about to come to an abrupt end.

Sitting upon the curb dining on a dog and Coke from a storefront eatery, you were forced to move when a Cadillac with NY plates squeezed in to park. The young driver jumped out to tell you he had just arrived from Woodstock, waving a NY tabloid, the lede, entire front page and much of the inside devoted to the event. He was not to be ignored. You weren't there. You weren't hip. He was. Yesterday. You had to read the news today. And listen to him. He was all alone and in P-town with his daddy's Caddy. It was time to tune in and turn on…or else. Oh, boy.

Ah, Commercial Street in Provincetown on a fine mid-August day in 1969. The eastern terminus of US 6 squeezes through a quaint New England fishing village curled up in the very tip of Cape Cod. A hamlet of narrow one-way streets and lanes with a great natural harbor, location of the Pilgrims first landing in the New World and populated by generations of stalwart Portuguese fishermen, gourmet restaurateurs, artists, writers—a haven for those with alternative life styles. Surrounded and isolated by endless miles of sand dunes, sea and beaches of the Cape Cod National Seashore. For ages it has been a refuge to escape the heat and hassles of the big city in summer. Had been. *Purple haze all in my brain…lately things they don't seem the same… actin' funny and I don't know why…'scuse me while I kiss the sky,*[1] booms out from the nearby T-shirt shop while you devour the tabloid news about Country Joe, Jimi, Janis, The Who.

Lined with stores of every description, Commercial Street winds through town, a one-way narrow main drag, packed with plenty of commercial action. Need a souvenir beach toy, an Italian Ice, the best lobsta roll in town, clothing or some primo blond Lebanese? It's here…or over there. A literal stream of humanity rolls past you. Station wagons full of family vacationers, *the cars crawl by all stuffed with eyes,*[2] an endless caravan of VW bugs and minibuses, a sharp looking biker crew with Québec plates rumbles through. Cruising the sidewalk a maritime mix of: surfers, scuba divers, recreational sailors, commercial fishermen, watercolor artists and rough trade trolling for business. In short, everyone from *everywhere.* Including the family dog.

Was Warhol there? Why not?

Whata yah guys smokin'?

You were actually shopping for a place to park.
You couldn't stay where you were…you only stopped for
a quick bite to eat and to read the paper. A tourist photo-
graphed you from a passing car, cracking Jim up. He pulled
out his camera and shot back…all the fresh air and sunshine
was blowin' his mind. But if you were going to join this
carnival you had to find a place to stash the ride. A popu-
lar problem. A map might help. Once obtained it was clear
that a major part of the local action centered on the docks…
complete with an appropriately large parking lot. *Sorry Full.*
Yeah…so where? Try up by the tower.

Rising from the highest point in town, the Pilgrim Monu-
ment is a 252-foot stack of granite modeled upon a tower in
Siena, Italy, or a Portuguese lighthouse, depending on whom
you ask. The tower is the focal point of this tourist extrav-
aganza, surrounded by a vast highly unattractive parking
area. Let's drive right into the belly of the beast! *Not so fast.*
Gated, monitored by a young woman who informs you that
as soon as some cars leave you may enter. You begin to feel

as if you are losing your street cred to common American automotive atrophy.

Parking fee gets you a free pass to the top of the tower…
Up for it?

Just one pass per vehicle, Pal. One of you has to pay admission…Yeah. Ok, we got it. Where's the elevator? None. You have to walk your lazy rock and roll asses up to the top. Mostly ramps…it's not bad. No pain…no gain. Welcome to the carnival.

God Damn! What a view! North, East, South, West…you guys breathed it all in like you never saw a clear day before. After commandeering two coin-operated binoculars you began to reconnoiter. You: Man people are still streaming into this town…Only one road, in…and out…[thought] I wonder if the same folks that packed the small costal towns in FL for the moon launch and then experimented with seeing how many people could cram into a cow pasture in the Catskills are now ending their historic summer with a street fair in P-Town? Could be. Was it the cheap gas or the Interstate system or the nice weather? Something, *something* was happening. The appreciation of the power of the people—

the shared communality between us. As people…not as a *people* but as brothers and sisters. An unorganized ground swell of freedom. A good economy, great clothes, cheap drugs, cold beer, cool shades, a celebration of what could be. A much needed respite from years of war. A cry for unity, for peace, for nature topped with the grooviest music ever! The summer of '69…man, you had to have been there to *feel* it.

And then it was gone. Forever. Like a dove lost in the wind …*poof.* Over.

Jim was studying the curvature of the Cape. Lighthouses dot the horizon. Out there, what's that? Far off in the distance over parched shrub and shimmering sand rises Highland Light. Perched on a spectacular bluff overlooking a vast curvature of beach…let's stop in the late afternoon as the sun is going down. Deal. A few hours of checking out the attractions in town were all you needed. Army/Navy/used clothing and junk in a carnivorous warehouse…you could have upgraded your boonie hat, but it was just getting real nice, fading and sporting an excellent band of perspiration. Somebody on the street had stuck a flower in it earlier that day. [Somehow you wandered into a fishery with the two largest tunas you ever saw] After pooling your cash Jim decided in a cinematographic maritime head that maybe you should go whale watching. *Sorry, all boats are full for the day. We have openings tomorrow morning at an ungodly hour. Hey, are you guys' brothers? In a band or something?*

So, where was this lighthouse? North Truro. Maybe six or eight miles out of town. Not far. A couple years ago you could climb it for a few bucks. A good place to shoot.

Let's roll.

You'd spend an hour or more taking in the sun, sea breeze, the deep cerulean sky, high cirrus clouds and crashing surf at the light before meandering back out to Route 6. Crank down the windows, pop in a tape. Traffic? Sure. *Dear Mr. Fantasy?* Perfect. You were cruising off the Cape unsuspectingly towards Altamont and Kent State.

The years go by.

Since 1969 Highland Light has been moved back 450 feet from its location on the bluffs overlooking the Atlantic. The ocean has taken yards of the bluff and scattered the sands to wherever they go…wherever they go. It's an all too common occurrence on the Outer Cape now. The most enduring photos of Woodstock became those of the audience, not the performers. And Provincetown did not sink into the sea from too many tourists…it is, however, now at risk from rising sea levels.

You never went back to the Cape together but Jim became a total sea freak. Totally. He learned to dive, became a Scuba instructor, moved to Cozumel to pursue an island life devoted to underwater photography, sun, sand, endless summer and peace.

People around the world have souvenir photos and videos riding Rays or posing with a Moray eel while diving with Jim.

And then *he* was gone. The sea had taken him. Sucked away by a riptide while boogie boarding during a day off with his wife and friends. A fucking *riptide* took down a man who spiritually respected the water, its inhabitants and its ecological importance. Boogie boarding.

The scattering of grains of sand.

The timeless lapping of the surf.

The smoky hints of Sandalwood.

The rip…rest in peace…my brother.

I'm driftin' and driftin' like a ship out on the sea…nobody seems to want me…except the wide and open sea.[3]

1 *Purple Haze, Jimi Hendrix; single release, 1967*
2 *Soul Kitchen, Jim Morrison; The Doors, 1967*
3 *Driftin' Blues, Paul Butterfield Blues Band; Live at Woodstock, 1969*

Summer Reflections

You are sitting in your favorite chair on the deck outside the kitchen. A gentle breeze washes over you this sunny afternoon while waiting for the lawn crew's arrival, nursing a gin and tonic in one hand as the other rubs the dog behind his ears. Life is good.

Surveying the backyard, your thoughts turn to the former long-time gardener and handyman, George. Originally hired by your family, he maintained the property for decades before advancing age and glaucoma finally put him out to pasture.

You never hired *anyone* to replace him. *He was irreplaceable,* you've said.

A crew comes now once a week to mow, edge, feed the lawns; maybe weed-wack a little, blow dust and clippings about and burn-up gasoline. They're interested in how quickly they can perform. They came recommended, do an Ok job and have many accounts…but don't engender much serendipity.

George was wedded to the property; slow, painstaking…an operator of hand tools, brooms, and rakes. He maintained a tidy shed at the end of the old greenhouse to accommodate his meticulously maintained collection of tools.
It was a different time.

George's legacy, however, is the high wall he constructed that separates the patio area from the rest of the property. Built from salvaged paving bricks and cobblestones that he unearthed somewhere. He had the vision to repurpose the refuse from old city streets to create a timeless artisanal wall. He painstaking selected, cleaned and soaked the pavers in water, then using small batches of mortar mixed by hand, transformed these materials into a thing of beauty. It looks as good now as when he built it in the late 1950s or very early '60s, or maybe sometime in the 17th century.

Solid. Rustic. European.

Juniper bushes originally planted along the wall have aged-out, replaced with tall reed grasses by the guys from the local nursery. They sway pleasantly in today's breeze, adding a soft kinetic motion to the garden. George never plant-ed grasses but you are sure he'd approve. He manicured the small patches of lawn around the wall and patio areas with a hand mower and edged with a trusty pair of shears. You can still hear the whine of the spinning blades as he pushed and pulled the mower over the lawn, and the brisk swish of the straw broom when he was finished. Vaguely, you recall the yard smelling sweeter after being freshly mowed in those days.

Completing a hot day of yard work, George would take note of his accomplishments, cigarette dangling from his mouth, garden hose in hand, he'd sprinkle and wash-down the walkways. Watering as if in a meditative state…caring for his charges.

You have an extensive sprinkler system now. Works like clockwork, timed to go on just before dawn. It never takes a break for a smoke or an iced drink or lunch. Never stops to chat. Efficient.

Your gaze returns to the wall. Stone, maybe marble, urns once sat along the top over-flowing with flowers by this time in the season. At some point they were removed and have long since disappeared…far too much work to move a step ladder around and maintain them you suppose. Someone, somewhere, must be using them, you bet. Still inhabiting a prominent position in this old world tableau is a calibrated sundial. *It's not going anywhere, you vow.*

Abruptly you are pulled back into the 21st century as the crew arrives—a couple hours late—and mowers chug off the trailer.

You hasten indoors, checking that all the windows are closed in hopes of mitigating some of the noise and preventing gasoline fumes from wafting throughout every nook and cranny of the house. Mission accomplished, you head into the kitchen settling in a chair overlooking the yard.

They'll be gone before the ice melts in this drink, you imagine, nursing a fresh gin and tonic in one hand as the other rubs the dog behind his ears.

Life is good.

The Park

As I sit contemplating autumn's spectacular splendor in
¬ Central Park,
I am mindful that I am residing in an oasis,
Within the heart of an urban jungle.
A bit of the countryside, we're often told, in the City.

Really?

This carefully managed bucolic preserve, resplendent with
stately trees, lagoons, reflecting ponds, the sound of water
softly flowing, fountains spraying, birds singing, squirrels
scampering and, of course, children shouting, is like the
countryside?

Well, yes, it has trees, but—

Really?

There are no bullet riddled road signs here.
No hulks of rusting automobiles, no high-tension towers
¬ strung with wires,

No weed filled abandoned rail yards. No dumps.

¬ No decaying towns.

No semis belching exhaust, No gaudy roadside attractions—
not even any billboards.

Really.

The park definitely is *not* the countryside.

But instead a well-designed nature conservatory

Not a natural history museum, (those have roofs and

¬ charge admission).

Rather, as a dynamic living organism.

The park could possibly be a noble endeavor intended

¬ to save us from civilization.

All the while being watched over like a hawk,

By its guardians, perched in the heart of

The Urban Jungle.

Twilight

I Wish I Could Write

I wish I could write a great poem today—
Something *really* cool.

I moved my 26 letters around…
Then moved them back,
Like a timid fool.

I mused on humanitarianism,
Nature and art
But came up empty!

A silent mind fart.

Then I worked on *love* for a little while.
A bit better.
A promising start.

Alas, love went nowhere,
I'm sad to say.
Moved all 26 back.

And, wrote off the day.

Cognitive Matters

As I age I have difficulty remembering some, not all,
¬ significant events from my past.

Some things in whole…some in part.

I remember my father's passing but not the date.

My Mom's death was on July 14, Bastille Day.

My sister and I pushed the cremation button together…
¬ I remember.

I have, however, forgotten much of my life.

Important matters too.

Leaving space for the new.

But the antithesis also holds true.

Some memories linger forever.

And I have lasting issues with some.

One in particular…

Visits me upon occasion—

Black velvet…with a breath of soft perfume.

My Heart (and Soul)

—1—

It's battered.
It's bruised.
Keeps me up at night.

The cardiologist said,
It was fine.
Watch the salt.

The physician said,
Vitals were good.
Watch the carbs.

The neurologist said,
No damage can be found.
Try homeopathy.

The holistic practitioner said,
Exercise and tea…
See a poet, not me.

The poet told me,
Please, have a seat.
Don't sit on the cat.
What's on your mind?

My heart feels battered,
Like pieces are missing.
But, I'm told I'm fine.

Oh, it's not your heart
That is the matter then.
It might be your soul.

Pieces—*may*—be missing,
Fissures often run deep
From long, long ago.
This messes with sleep.

What can I do?

Write a story,
Do a book,
Maybe a poem?

About what?

Whatever you like.
Whenever you like.
I don't have to see it,
Unless you like.

Just write.

Repeat as often as you can.
It may not help.
But it certainly won't hurt.

Return whenever
Regarding this damage
But, please…please, call me first.

What do I owe you?

Oh, I'm a poet, you see.
Perhaps some repartee,
Maybe coffee or tea.

That's the usual fee.

Thank you, I'll be back.
Grabbed my coat and my hat
Out through the door,
Watching for the cat.

—2—

As I fell into a rhythm, tapping the worn bluestone sidewalks under my feet, I admired the sun, this chilly April afternoon, casting long shadows from aged sycamores upon the weathered brownstones. While my thoughts turned to what traumas could have done so much damage to my soul.

Then pausing in my tracks, I turned and descended a narrow flight of rusting stairs, ducking into the entrance of this tiny Thai place—looking for something comforting to eat.

I was greeted promptly, led quickly to a seat, presented with a menu and a pot of hot Jasmine tea. As I was perusing the entrees while unwrapping my sticks the mind began to wander…what on earth, if anything, could I ever create?

Temple of the Holy Word

[I picked you up one night when you looked like you needed
a lift. I asked you where you were going? You said, "Wher-
ever I was headed…just make it quick."]

I said, "OK."
Some go this way.
Some go write.
I'll be cruising straight
Down the middle of the Pike.
Past each avenue
A through Z.

That's all right?

You quipped, "So anyway,
Out past Z is Coney.
Keep that in your mind.
You're headed to the Temple?"

Yes, of the Holy Word.
Please, remember when

We finally get there,
We haven't actually arrived.

You said, "Yes, that's the place!
Let's go for a ride."

We flew down that Pike,
Past each avenue—
The destination
just out of our view.

When in fact you do enter…
Passing *slowly* through the doors…
You'll sense the muses chanting.
With some luck, you'll catch their call…
…no hate…no fear…poets are welcome here…
…no hate…no fear…poets are welcome here…
*…say it **loud** and say it clear…*
…no hate…no fear…poets are welcome here…
…no hate…no fear…poets are welcome here…

The Nonsense Worshippers Highway

We were far past Logic,
Rhyme and Reason
Barreling along the
Incomprehensible
Dialogue Highway
Seeking any story
To illuminate an
Event looming
Ahead

The signs were there as
We stopped for a light
At the corner of Avenue Q
And don't turn on right

It looked like a circus
Had come to town
The clowns were parading
About and around

Conspiracies were
Arising anyone could join in
Just bring some meth
A flag, sign and a friend

This was different than
The old times by far…
No pennons of peace, love
Or end of war

We listened to orators
For hours on end
Unable to relate
To anything they said

As hate welled in the crowd
We ducked out to
The highway back home
Past the wreckage we witnessed
Of sanity and reason
Well and good

Back to the reality
That we all understood

I will note, however,
The evidence was *clear*
It wasn't clowns in town
But rather—Jokers

Lost and Found

Found two phone numbers
In the back of a drawer.
One may have been your sister's,
The other your mom's?
An old tarnished set of keys,
Not valid anymore.
And a faded greeting card…
To me—from you.

What should I do?

Bury everything?
Return it back to the earth?
Enabling these relics
To bond with you?
Or light a fire,
A small ritualistic pyre?
Is *any* of this
Important now?

[I thought out loud.]

Moved it all to the trash.
That's when I heard from you.
Been waiting for you to find this, Silly.
I'm wondering, how are you?

I'm fine…I lied.

So, I rescued everything
From certain oblivion.
Sealed all in an envelope.
Placed it gently back
Into my drawer—
Way, way, back…back forever…
Forever in—
My Lost and Found.

You Have a Nice Pace

I walked five laps for you today,
Through the park on an
Early autumn day.

I didn't listen to music.
I didn't check my phone.
I walked in silence, with you—
All alone.

I pictured your smile,
Your long flowing hair.

And I recalled the first time,
When you passed me by,
Oblivious to all things—
Even I?

I walked five laps *with* you today,
Like some character,
In a poem or play.

I wish that I could do this.
I wish that *we* could do this.
I wish that we could do this—
Every day.

No One Told Us

They said that we were
Meant for each other

We would always be
Partners…forever

No one warned us though
How tragically short

Our lives forever
Would forever be.

December's Child

This is my time
I'm a son of December
A man of ice and snow
Born during a blizzard
Many, many years ago

The bitter winds
Welcomed me to this world
Amid urban decay
By a great frozen lake
On a late autumn day

But, I'm lucky
I blew in with the wind
Those many years ago
My twin would not arrive—
I entered this world

Alone

About the Author

Jim Seegert has been a frequent reader and featured performer of both poetry and spoken word in the New York City metropolitan area, principally with the Performance Poet's Association throughout Queens/Long Island, and the Phoenix Reading Series in the West Village, among others.

Following his retirement to the Hudson Valley, Jim has become a regular on the Calling All Poet's (CAPs) Zoom events and as a live performer at Lit/Lit in Beacon, NY. He still enjoys an intimate read in smaller venues such as a library, park or bookstore.

"Writing is what I pour my creative energy into these days," Seegert a graduate of the prestigious Cleveland Institute of Art declares, "What I learned wasn't only artistic techniques but, even more importantly, to experiment, to think, to be creative."

Jim survived a career in network television graphics and as a commercial artist in Cleveland and NYC.

A decade of Jim's spoken performances are captured here—chronicling our popular culture during the last half century. Odes to music, poetry, lifestyles, friendships and the fickle winds of change are showcased in his unique non-judgmental, conversational manner.

Fresh Light is Seegert's debut anthology.

Addendum

The author arrived in NYC in 1981

He lived downtown

On Water Street

In a loft

Near the Bridge Café

With the unceasing hum

Of bridge traffic

Serenading him 24/7

He wasn't there long

The neighborhood was

Up-and-coming

About to be cleaned-up

The artists and musicians

Kicked out

The fragrance on Sunday evenings

Of melting ice dumped on the streets from

Fish deliveries to the Fulton Market gone

Replaced by throngs of day-trippers

From Queens, Kansas, Katmandu…

A gallery featuring pictures

Of the Brooklyn Bridge

And the neighborhood's ancient

Cobblestone streets

Now occupied his former residence

The *Seaport Museum* had arrived

He managed to stay in the City

For forty more years

Until the pandemic

Before retiring upstate

To the Hudson Valley

His mind, on the other hand,

Continues to wander…

Acknowledgments

I would like to thank all the editors who have included my work in their publications. (Alpha order)

Breath of Spring, CAPs Poetry 25th Anniversary Anthology, March 2024

Cognitive Matters, Verse-Virtual, July 2023

I Wish I Could Write, Performance Poets Association Review, vol. #24

Lost and Found, Verse-Virtual, January 2024

Music Therapy, Verse-Virtual, July 2024

My Résumé, Tamarind Review, June 2021

Temple of the Holy Word, Performance Poets Association Review, vol. #23

You Have a Nice Pace, Performance Poets Association Review, vol. #22

Special thanks to Ron Kolm for permission to use his memoir *The Bookstore Book* in Midwinter Trip